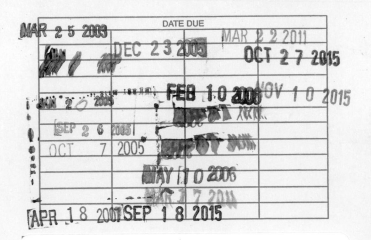

363.2
GRE

T 32798

Green, Michael.

SWAT teams

AR
RL
5.0
PTS
0.5

CASTI

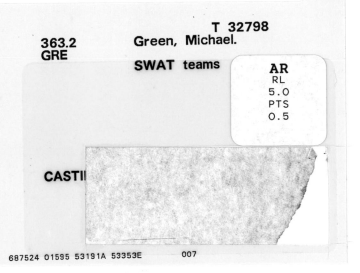

Law Enforcement

SWAT Teams

by Michael Green

Content Consultant:
Ben Tisa
Special Weapons and Tactics Instructor
Federal Bureau of Investigation (retired)

CAPSTONE BOOKS
an imprint of Capstone Press
Mankato, Minnesota

Capstone Books are published by Capstone Press
151 Good Counsel Drive, P.O. Box 669, Mankato, Minnesota 56002
http://www.capstone-press.com

Library of Congress Cataloging-in-Publication Data
Green, Michael, 1952-
    SWAT teams/by Michael Green.
    p. cm. -- (Law enforcement)
    Includes bibliographical references and index.
    Summary: Provides an introduction to police departments' special
weapons and tactics (SWAT) teams, including their history, organization,
functions, responsibilities, weapons and equipment.
    ISBN 1-56065-758-8
    1. Police--United States--Special weapons and tactics units--Juvenile
literature. [1. Police--Special weapons and tactics units.] I. Title. II. Series:
Green, Michael, 1952- Law enforcement.
HV7922.G724 1998
363.2'32--dc21

                                        97-40394
                                          CIP
                                           AC

Editorial credits:
Editor, Timothy Larson; cover design, Timothy Halldin; photo research,
    Michelle L. Norstad
Photo credits:
Michael Green, cover, 10, 12, 15, 28, 30, 47
Hans Haberstadt, 36
Samuel M. Katz, 4, 6, 18, 20, 26, 34, 41
New York City Police Department, 8
Leslie O'Shaugnessy, 16, 23, 24, 33, 38

2 3 4 5 6 04 03 02 01 00

Table of Contents

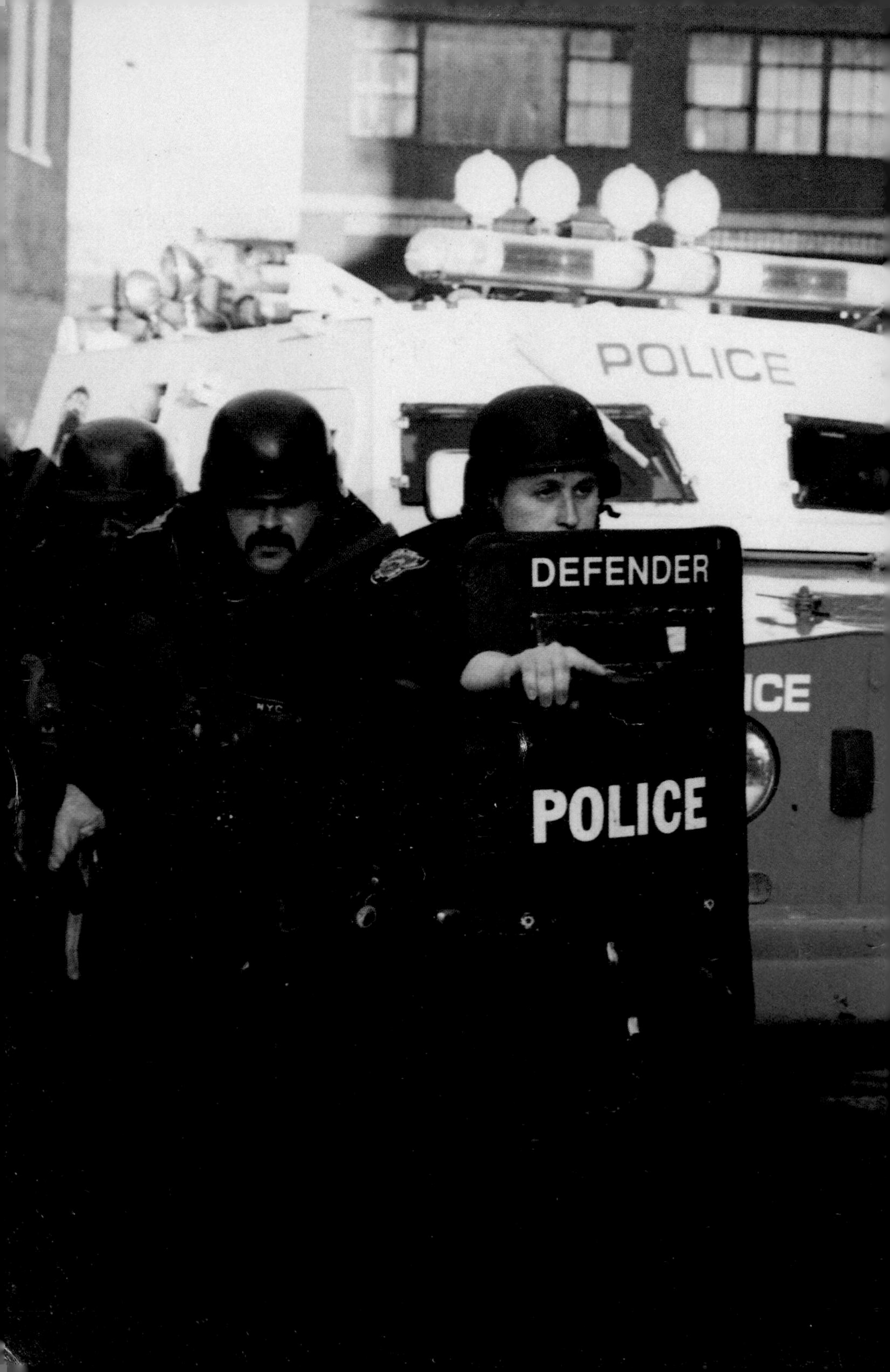
POLICE
DEFENDER
POLICE
ICE

Chapter 1

SWAT Teams

SWAT teams are highly trained police units. A unit is a small group within a larger group. SWAT stands for Special Weapons and Tactics. Tactics are actions aimed at solving problems.

SWAT team members are weapons and tactics specialists. A specialist is a person trained for a particular job. SWAT team members use their special weapons, tactics, and training to protect the public. They handle police emergencies. An emergency is a sudden and risky situation.

Police send SWAT teams to many kinds of police emergencies. The emergencies often involve one or more heavily armed suspects. A suspect is a person believed to have committed a crime. SWAT teams work on hostage situations. A hostage is a person held against his or her will.

SWAT team members use special weapons and training to protect the public.

Law enforcement agencies use different names for their SWAT teams.

SWAT teams perform many jobs. They come to robberies that are in progress. They help guard government officials. They help stop terrorists. A terrorist is a person who tries to get what he or she wants by threatening or harming others. SWAT teams also patrol high-crime areas.

SWAT Team Names

SWAT teams can be part of city, county, or state law enforcement agencies. A law enforcement agency is an office or department that makes sure people obey laws. Police departments and sheriffs departments are examples of law enforcement agencies.

Law enforcement agencies use different names for their SWAT teams. The names include Emergency Service Unit and Emergency Response Team. They also include Mobile Emergency Response Group and Equipment (MERGE) and Tactical Response Team.

SWAT Team Beginnings

The New York Police Department (NYPD) had one of the earliest specially trained police units. In the mid-1880s, the NYPD set up small units of police officers. The department called these units strong-arm squads. The squads fought criminal gangs. Police clubs were their only weapons.

By the 1920s, criminal gangs had grown in size and power. The gangs bought handguns, rifles, and submachine guns. A submachine gun is a light gun that fires rapidly. The criminal gangs fought one another on New York City streets. Many innocent people died.

In 1925, the NYPD formed the Emergency Service Unit (ESU). The department also formed the Gunman's Squad as part of the unit. The

The Gunman's Squad patrolled New York City streets in green trucks like this one.

squad included 60 heavily armed police officers. The officers had handguns, rifles, and submachine guns. They worked on cases involving criminal gangs. They patrolled the city in green trucks.

Other large police departments formed early SWAT team units. These units also worked to stop criminal gangs.

Growth and Change

The Gunman's Squad is a good example of how the early SWAT teams grew and changed. This squad became the Mobile Security Unit (MSU) in the late 1940s. The new unit was larger than the old unit. It continued to fight criminal gang activity.

The MSU changed in the late 1960s. More people lived in New York City. The number of murders and robberies increased. The MSU formed the Stakeout Squad to fight the increase in crime.

The NYPD's best police officers joined the Stakeout Squad. Each member was a skilled police officer and marksman. A marksman is a person skilled at aiming and shooting guns. The Stakeout Squad worked on difficult cases. It helped the NYPD lower the number of murders in the city.

In the 1970s, Stakeout Squad officers learned new skills. They learned anti-terrorist tactics and

Today's LAPD SWAT team members receive special weapons training like they did in the past.

special weapons skills. Officers also learned how to rescue hostages. The skills helped them fight terrorists. In the 1980s, the squad was taken over by the Emergency Service Unit. Today, this unit controls all NYPD SWAT operations.

The LAPD SWAT TEAM

The Los Angeles Police Department (LAPD) changed law enforcement around the country in the 1960s. Los Angeles police officers found themselves outgunned by criminals. The criminals had powerful weapons. So the LAPD formed a specially trained and armed police unit to protect people.

The LAPD named the unit the Special Weapons and Tactics (SWAT) team. Team members received special weapons training. They also learned how to handle police emergencies. The team was very successful.

Other police and sheriffs departments saw the success of the Los Angeles Police Department's SWAT team. Many departments formed their own SWAT teams.

Today, special training centers in the United States train and organize many SWAT teams. The centers teach SWAT team members tactics and weapons skills.

Chapter 2

SWAT Team Officers

There are more than 17,000 police departments in the United States. Many have either full-time or part-time SWAT teams. Many SWAT team officers work more than 40 hours each week. Most officers are on call 24 hours a day. On call means ready to work at any time.

SWAT team officers perform hard and risky work. They risk their lives each time they go out on a police emergency. Police officers are not ordered to join SWAT teams. Instead, they volunteer. Volunteer means to offer to do a job.

Training

SWAT team officers receive special training. Large police departments usually conduct their

Police officers volunteer for SWAT team duty.

own training. Officers in small units receive SWAT training from large units or from training centers.

The federal government also trains large and small SWAT teams. The FBI operates an advanced training school at Quantico, Virginia. The U.S. Army and U.S. Marine Corps also conduct training classes.

During training, officers learn through classes and field work. Officers learn about crime situations and SWAT tactics. Officers learn about different weapons and practice using them.

Officers also receive other training. Many officers learn advanced first aid. First aid is early medical help. Some officers learn to be sharpshooters. A sharpshooter is a marksman skilled at hitting small or distant targets.

Some officers learn how to handle and use tear gas. Tear gas is a gas that causes a painful burning feeling in the eyes and lungs. Tear gas disables suspects. Other officers learn communication skills. Communication is the

During training, officers learn SWAT tactics.

sharing of information. Communication allows officers to calm suspects by talking to them.

Special Teams

Most SWAT teams include three kinds of smaller specialized teams. They include negotiator teams, containment teams, and entry teams. Each team

Negotiators listen and talk to suspects during police emergencies.

performs a different kind of job. Sometimes only one specialized team works on an emergency. Other times, all three teams work together.

Negotiator Teams

Negotiators are communications experts. They listen and talk to suspects during police emergencies. Negotiators use words to reason with suspects and solve problems. They often work on hostage situations. They try to convince suspects to free their hostages and surrender. Surrender means to give up peacefully.

Negotiators have to be calm. They must think carefully about each word they say. They do not want to upset a suspect. This could cause a suspect to harm hostages.

Negotiators may spend hours talking with suspects. Sometimes they use phones and talk from a safe distance. Other times they talk with suspects in person. In these cases, suspects will often talk only if negotiators do not have weapons.

Containment Teams

Containment teams control and contain crime scenes. Contain means to hold in. They make sure innocent people do not become involved in a situation. They also make sure suspects do not escape. Containment officers make observations and report what they see to their leaders. Sometimes they have to shoot at suspects.

Entry teams enter and search buildings.

Containment officers take different positions at a crime scene. They choose locations that help them see what is happening. Some may crouch on rooftops. Some may stand in doorways.

Others may take positions behind cars. Containment officers are patient. They control their emotions while under pressure. Containment officers also think carefully before they shoot. Careless shots could hurt innocent people or lead to deadly shoot-outs.

Entry Teams

Entry teams enter and search buildings. Their job is to find and capture suspects in the buildings. They also try to locate and rescue hostages.

Sometimes entry team officers must secure crime scenes. This means they prevent suspects from harming others or killing themselves. Entry team officers also prevent suspects from escaping or destroying evidence. Evidence is facts or objects that help prove guilt.

Entry team officers can break through locked or barricaded entrances quickly. Barricaded means blocked. The officers use tools to break windows and push through doors. Quick entries allow officers to catch suspects off guard. This makes entry operations safer.

Chapter 3

SWAT Team Operations

All SWAT teams try to resolve police emergencies as quickly and safely as possible. They want to capture suspects without harming the public, hostages, or the suspects.

SWAT teams work carefully during their operations to reduce chances of harm or death. SWAT teams use different tactics to reach these goals. They try peaceful tactics first.

Peaceful Tactics

Waiting is one peaceful tactic SWAT teams use. SWAT teams sometimes wait for hours before they take more forceful action. Waiting gives suspects a chance to think about what they are

SWAT teams try to resolve police emergencies with peaceful tactics.

doing. It also gives suspects time to think about what may happen to them. Sometimes suspects surrender after they have time to think.

Persuasion and negotiation are other tactics SWAT teams use. Persuasion is trying to change a person's mind. Negotiation is talking to reach an agreement. The goal of these tactics is to talk suspects into surrendering without harming others.

Many times, SWAT teams use other tactics in combination with persuasion and negotiation. For example, teams may cut the heat or air conditioning in buildings where suspects are. They may constantly ring doorbells or call suspects on the phone. These tactics make the suspects nervous. Sometimes they make criminals more willing to surrender.

Forceful Tactics

SWAT teams change their tactics if more force is needed. They use forceful tactics when negotiation and persuasion tactics fail. They also use forceful tactics if the lives of hostages and officers are in danger.

Forceful tactics include the use of tear gas.

Forceful tactics include using tear gas, storming buildings, and attacking with sharpshooters. Tear gas is the least forceful of these tactics.

Tear Gas

SWAT team officers often use tear gas as their first forceful tactic. Officers shoot cans of tear gas through windows and doorways with tear gas

Entry teams meet at staging areas to check equipment and to go over plans.

guns. The tear gas makes suspects' eyes burn and swell. The suspects have a hard time breathing in rooms filled with tear gas.

Tear gas often disables suspects. This allows officers to arrest suspects safely. Other times, tear gas forces suspects to surrender.

Entering a Building

Sometimes officers must enter buildings to try to capture suspects. Entry teams meet at a staging area before entering a building. A staging area is a safe area near a building that officers plan to enter. Entry team members check their equipment and weapons at staging areas. They also go over their plans for entry.

Next, the entry teams enter buildings. They must often break through barricaded doors and windows. Once inside, officers search rooms and hallways. They search until they locate suspects and hostages.

Entry team officers try to capture and disarm suspects. Disarm means to take away a person's weapons. Many times suspects surrender when they see entry teams. Sometimes suspects shoot at the officers. The officers shoot back.

Entry team officers often turn captured suspects over to arrest teams. Arrest teams arrest captured suspects. They make sure nothing goes wrong during arrests. They may also help hostages out of buildings.

Sharpshooting teams include observers and sharpshooters.

Sharpshooting Teams

Sharpshooters may have to shoot suspects. This may become necessary if suspects try to harm hostages, officers, or innocent bystanders.

Sharpshooters may receive orders to shoot suspects in these situations.

Many SWAT units have sharpshooting teams. Each team includes two officers. One officer works as an observer. The other works as a sharpshooter.

Sharpshooting Team Operations

Sharpshooting teams choose locations that give them clear views of suspects. Both members examine crime scenes from their location.

Observers provide information about suspects to sharpshooters and SWAT team leaders. The information includes descriptions of suspects, their weapons, and their positions in buildings. Observers' information helps sharpshooters make sure they do not shoot at innocent people.

Sharpshooters stay calm and keep their weapons aimed at suspects. Orders to shoot a suspect can come at any time during an operation.

Chapter 4

Special Weapons

SWAT team officers use special weapons. Many of the weapons are powerful guns. At crime scenes, the weapons help the officers protect themselves and capture suspects. But SWAT team members do not use their weapons unless peaceful tactics fail.

Different weapons are useful in different situations. Some weapons are useful in short-range situations. Other weapons are useful in long-range situations.

Stun Guns and Rubber Bullets

Sometimes SWAT team officers use impact weapons. Impact weapons disable suspects

SWAT team officers use powerful weapons.

Sometimes SWAT team officers use submachine guns.

without killing them. These weapons fire rubber
or plastic bullets. Using impact weapons reduces
the risk of harm to hostages and the public.

Sometimes officers use stun guns. A stun gun
is a device that delivers an electric shock. The
shock stuns suspects.

Semi-automatic Handguns

Most SWAT team officers carry semi-automatic
handguns. A semi-automatic handgun is a
powerful gun that fires bullets quickly. These

handguns are short-range weapons. They work best for targets within 25 yards (23 meters).

Semi-automatic handguns hold 14 to 17 rounds in each magazine. A round is a bullet. A magazine is a metal or plastic case that fits inside a gun. Magazines allow officers to reload their handguns quickly.

Shotguns

Sometimes SWAT team officers use shotguns. A shotgun is a powerful gun with a long barrel. Shotguns are mainly short-range weapons. They may be single-shot or semi-automatic weapons. Shotguns fire large bullets called shells.

SWAT teams often use the Benelli M3 Super 90 shotgun. This shotgun is a semi-automatic. It holds up to seven shells stored in a magazine.

Submachine Guns

SWAT teams use submachine guns during shoot-outs with heavily armed suspects. Submachine guns fire rapidly but are not easy to aim.

SWAT team submachine guns can fire single or multiple rounds. They fire multiple rounds in short and long bursts. A short burst is a quick series of two or three rounds. A long burst is a quick series of four to eight rounds.

Many SWAT teams use the Heckler and Koch MP-5 submachine gun. Most MP-5s have magazines that hold 30 rounds. The MP-5 can fire 30 shots in just two seconds.

Standard Rifle

SWAT teams use different rifles in different situations. Rifles give officers dependable aim, fire power, and range. The M-16 is the standard SWAT team rifle.

The M-16 is light. This makes it easy to carry and use. The M-16 has a dependable range of 50 to 200 yards (46 to 183 meters). Each magazine for the M-16 holds up to 30 rounds. These features make the rifle useful in many situations.

High-Powered Rifles

SWAT team officers use high-powered rifles for long-distance shooting. Containment officers and sharpshooters use high-powered rifles to improve their shots.

High-powered rifles fire high-powered rounds. They are large rifles with long barrels. They have telescopes on them. A telescope is an instrument that makes distant objects seem larger and closer.

SWAT team officers use high-powered rifles for long-distance shots.

Telescopes help sharpshooters aim their rifles. High-powered rifles have ranges up to several hundred yards.

Fifty-caliber rifles are the largest high-powered rifles SWAT teams use. These rifles weigh up to 40 pounds (18 kilograms) and are at least five feet (1.5 meters) long. The rifles shoot rounds powerful enough to punch through metal and concrete. Officers use these rifles to shoot at suspects inside buildings.

Helmet

Armored Vest

SWAT Team

Chapter 5

Equipment and Dogs

SWAT team officers use different kinds of equipment. The equipment ranges from clothing to helicopters. Officers also work with police dogs. The dogs and equipment help make SWAT team operations easier and safer.

Uniforms

Many SWAT team officers wear black or dark blue uniforms. During operations, the uniforms help SWAT team officers identify each other.

Sometimes SWAT team officers wear camouflage uniforms. Camouflage uniforms have coloring that makes officers blend in with their surroundings. Many camouflage uniforms are

Many SWAT team officers wear black or dark blue uniforms.

SWAT team officers use battering rams to break down doors.

green and brown. These uniforms help officers stay hidden from suspects.

Armored Vests and Shields

All SWAT team officers wear armored vests. Armor is a protective covering. Armored vests can protect officers from gunshots. Officers wear two kinds of armored vests. One kind fits over uniforms. The other kind fits under uniforms.

Entry team officers often use armored shields in addition to their armored vests. The shields are made of lightweight armor. They provide added protection against gunshots and small explosions.

Goggles and Gas Masks

Many SWAT team officers wear goggles. Goggles are protective glasses that fit tightly around the upper face and eyes. They protect officers' eyes from dirt, dust, and smoke.

Some SWAT teams use night vision goggles. Night vision goggles let SWAT team officers see in the dark. The goggles are useful during night operations or inside dark buildings.

SWAT team officers wear gas masks when they use tear gas. A gas mask keeps a person from breathing gas. Gas masks help entry teams work in areas where tear gas is present.

Entry Tools

Entry team officers often need tools to get into barricaded buildings. Basic tools include ropes and ladders. Tools can also include battering rams, sledge hammers, and axes. A battering ram is a heavy metal tube. Officers use battering rams to force open doors.

Entry teams recently started using small amounts of explosives. The explosives can blow holes in doors and walls. But the explosives present little danger to SWAT team members and suspects.

Helicopters
Some SWAT teams use helicopters. Helicopters carry SWAT teams to emergencies located in hard to reach places like rooftops.

Helicopters also let officers examine crime scenes from the air. This helps them plan their operations.

Walkie Talkies and Telephones
Communication is important to SWAT team officers. Officers often use walkie talkies. Walkie talkies are small two-way radios. Officers use walkie talkies to tell each other what is happening during an operation.

Sometimes SWAT teams use telephones to talk with suspects. Telephones also let team members speak to other people during operations.

SWAT Team Dogs
Many large SWAT teams use police dogs. Police dogs work with some SWAT officers as K-9 teams. K-9 is short for canine. Canine means dog. Most police dogs are German shepherds.

Police dogs help officers find suspects. The dogs follow suspects' scents to the suspects'

Some SWAT teams use police dogs and helicopters.

hiding places. Police dogs also chase and stop escaping suspects. They often stop suspects by biting the suspects' arms and legs.

Facing the Risks

SWAT team duty is challenging and risky work. Officers risk death each time they work on a police emergency.

Many officers volunteer for SWAT team duty because they like challenge and excitement. But most SWAT team officers volunteer because they want to protect the public.

Words to Know

armor (AR-mur)—a protective metal or plastic covering

barricaded (BAIR-uh-kay-duhd)—blocked

communication (kuh-myoo-nuh-KAY-shun)—the sharing of information

disarm (diss-ARM)—to take away a person's weapons

emergency (i-MUR-juhn-see)—a sudden and risky situation

hostage (HOSS-tij)—a person held against his or her will

magazine (MAG-uh-zeen)—a metal or plastic case that holds bullets and fits inside a gun

marksman (MARKS-muhn)—a person skilled at aiming and shooting guns

negotiation (ni-goh-shee-AY-shun)—talking to reach an agreement

on call (ON KAHL)—ready to work at any time

persuasion (per-SWAY-zhuhn)—trying to change a person's mind

sharpshooter (SHARP-shoo-tur)—a marksman skilled at hitting small or distant targets

specialist (SPESH-uh-list)—a person trained for a particular job

surrender (suh-REN-dur)—to give up peacefully

suspect (SUHS-pekt)—a person believed to have committed a crime

SWAT (SWAHT)—Special Weapons and Tactics

tactics (TAK-tics)—actions aimed at solving problems

tear gas (TIHR GASS)—a gas that causes a burning feeling in the eyes and lungs

telescope (TEL-uh-skope)—an instrument that makes distant objects seem larger and closer

terrorist (TER-ur-ist)—a person who tries to get what he or she wants by threatening or harming others

To Learn More

Cohen, Paul and Shari Cohen. *Careers in Law Enforcement and Security.* New York: Rosen Publishing Group, 1995.

Davis, Mary L. *Working in Law and Justice.* Exploring Careers. Minneapolis: Lerner Publications, 1999.

Green, Michael. *Bomb Detection Squads.* Mankato, Minn.: Capstone Books, 1998.

George, Charles and Linda George. *Police Dogs.* Mankato, Minn.: Capstone Books, 1998.

Useful Addresses

Federal Bureau of Investigation (FBI)
Attn: Public Affairs Office
J. Edgar Hoover FBI Building
10th Street and Pennsylvania Avenue NW
Washington, DC 20535

New York Police Department
Attn: Public Affairs Office
One Police Plaza
New York, NY 10038

San Jose Police Department
Attn: Public Affairs Office
201 W. Mission Street
San Jose, CA 95110

Internet Sites

Florida SWAT Association
http://sundial.sundial.net/swat/

Police Dog Homepages
http://www.best.com/~policek9/index.htm

The Police Officer's Internet Directory
http://www.officer.com/

Welcome to PoliceScanner.Com
http://www.policescanner.com/

SWAT team officers risk death each time they work on a police emergency.

Index